P9-DMM-635

WITHDRAWN

Ready for School

We Are a Team

Sharon Gordon

We are a team.

We work together.

We are a team.

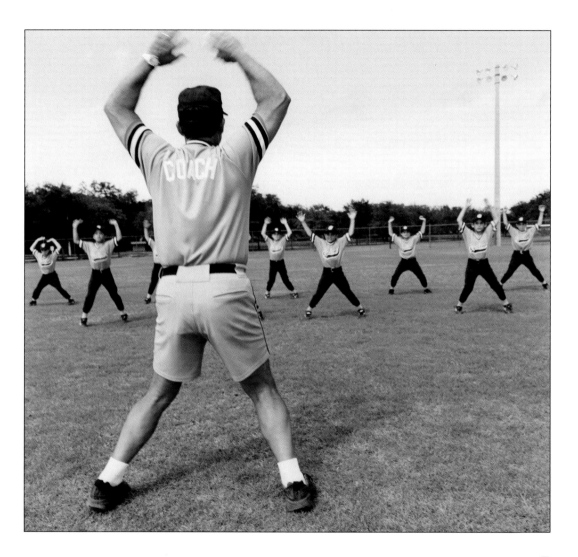

We make a plan.

We are a team.

We do our jobs.

We are a team.

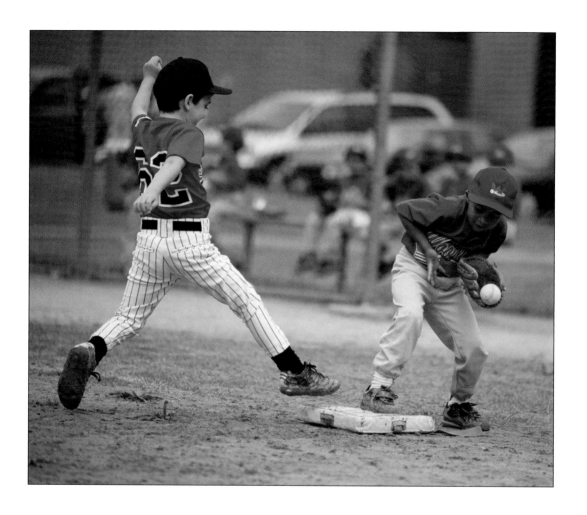

We take turns.

We are a team.

We do our best.

We are a team.

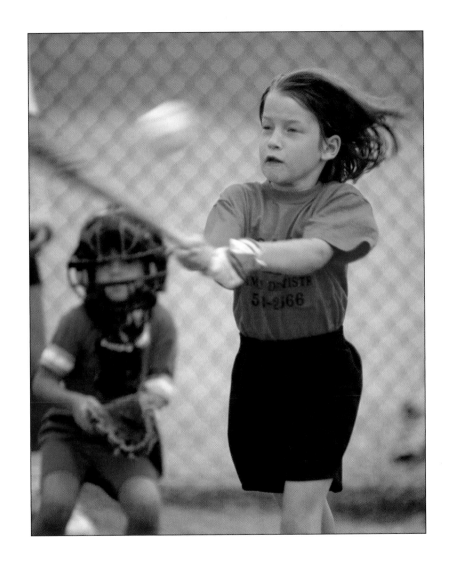

We help each other.

We are a team.

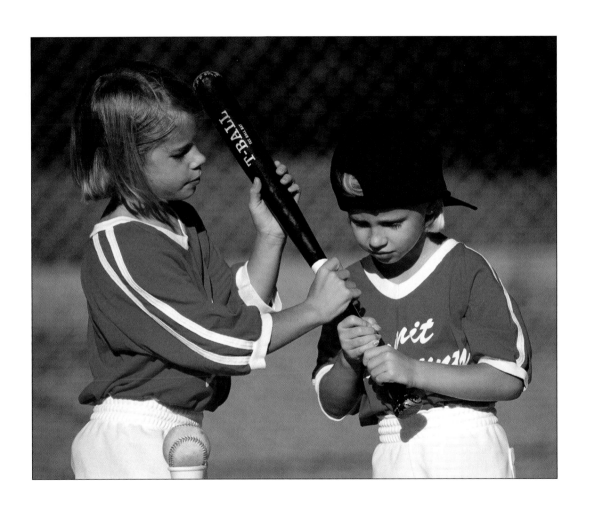

We cheer.

We are a team.

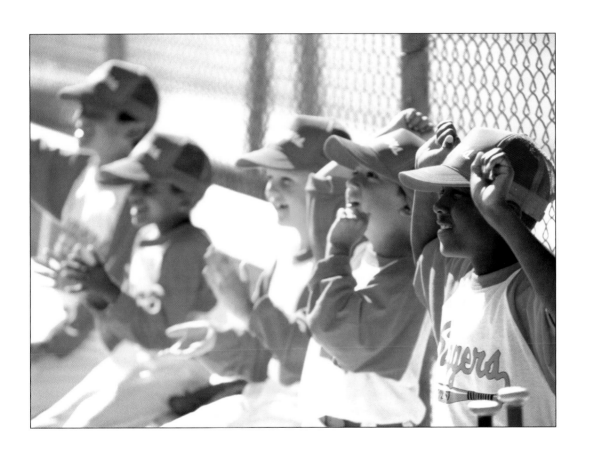

We are friends.

We are a team!

We Are a Team

best

cheer

friends

help

20

jobs

plan

take turns

work

Index

Page numbers in **boldface** are illustrations.

best, 12, **13**, **20**

cheer, 16, **17**, **20**

friends, 18, **19**, **20**

help, 14, **15**, **20**

jobs, 8, **9**, **21**

plan, 6, **7**, **21**

take turns, 10, **11**, **21**
team, 2, **3**

work, 4, **5**, **21**

About the Author

Sharon Gordon has written many books for young children. She has always worked as an editor. Sharon and her husband Bruce have three children, Douglas, Katie, and Laura, and one spoiled pooch, Samantha. They live in Midland Park, New Jersey.

With thanks to Nanci Vargus, Ed.D. and
Beth Walker Gambro, reading consultants

Marshall Cavendish Benchmark
Marshall Cavendish
99 White Plains Road
Tarrytown, New York 10591-9001
www.marshallcavendish.us

Text copyright © 2006 by Marshall Cavendish Corporation

All rights reserved. No part of this book may be reproduced or utilized in any form or
by any means electronic or mechanical, including photocopying, recording, or by any information storage and
retrieval system, without written permission from the copyright holders.

Library of Congress Cataloging-in-Publication Data

Gordon, Sharon.
We are a team / by Sharon Gordon.
p. cm. — (Bookworms. Ready for school)
Summary: "Demonstrates the importance of teamwork"—Provided by publisher.
ISBN 0-7614-1994-2
1. Sports for children—Juvenile literature. 2. Teamwork (Sports)—Juvenile literature.
3. Cooperativeness—Juvenile literature. I. Title. II. Series.

GV709.2.G67 2005
796'.082—dc22
2005007888

Photo Research by Anne Burns Images

Cover Photo by *SuperStock*/Banana Stock

The photographs in this book are used with permission and through the courtesy of:
Corbis: pp. 1, 11, 21 (bottom l) LWA-Dann Tardif; pp. 3, 9, 21 (top l) Ariel Skelley; pp. 5, 21 (bottom r) Patrick Giardino;
pp. 13, 20 (top l) Kevin Fleming; pp. 15, 17, 19, 20 (top r), 20 (bottom l), 20 (bottom r) Royalty Free.
SuperStock: pp. 7, 21 (top r) Kevin Radford.

Printed in Malaysia
1 3 5 6 4 2